APPLES

For Maria

The author wishes to express his appreciation to Jennifer Halsey, of the Halsey Farm in Watermill, New York; Louis Amsler, of Richcter's Orchard in East Northport, New York; and Richard Holmberg, of Holmberg's Orchards in Gales Ferry, Connecticut; and the folks at B. F. Clyde's Cider Mill, in Old Mystic, Connecticut. All generously shared their considerable knowledge. Martin C. Goffinet, of Cornell University's Department of Horticultural Sciences at the New York State Agricultural Experiment Station, was kind enough to provide the extraordinary photos on pages 16 and 17. And special thanks to Mia Goncalves and Colin Harrington, who posed for me.

Atheneum Books for Young Readers
An imprint of Simon & Schuster Children's Publishing Division
1230 Avenue of the Americas
New York, New York 10020

Book design by Sonia Chaghatzbanian.
The text of this book is set in Mrs Eaves.

Printed in Hong Kong

First Edition

2 4 6 8 10 9 7 5 3 1

Library of Congress Cataloging-in-Publication Data
Robbins, Ken.
Apples / text and pictures by Ken Robbins.—1st ed.
p.   cm.
ISBN 0-689-83024-6
Summary: Describes how apples are grown, harvested, and used,
and details facts about apples in history, literature, and our daily lives.
[1. Apples—Juvenile literature. 2. Apples.] I. Title.
SB363 .R62 2002
634/.11—dc21   2001033764

APPLES

TEXT AND PICTURES BY
Ken Robbins

Atheneum Books for Young Readers
New York London Toronto Sydney Singapore

An apple

is a wonderful thing—a perfect handful of portable food, wrapped in a package of its very own skin.

Apples, of course, are a kind of fruit. They are round and shiny, delicious and sweet, crisp to the bite, and they grow on trees. People have been growing them for thousands of years.

Apples can be red or yellow, or they can be green.
Sometimes they can be all three.

You can grow apple trees from apple seeds, but you never know what kind of apples will grow. That's why in most orchards, the apple trees aren't ever grown from seeds.

Instead, a branch from a tree that makes a particular kind of apple is joined, or grafted, onto the trunk of a small tree that already has roots. The two grow together when they're planted in the ground. And the result is a tree that produces the same kind of apple, year after year.

In ten years the planted tree is big enough and ready to grow fruit. The growing season starts with pruning the trees—cutting away dead branches.

In the spring the trees in the apple orchard burst into bloom. Some have pink flowers, some have white.

Soon the orchardist sets out hives of bees in the orchard. Some keep bees themselves—others pay a beekeeper to bring them to the orchard when they are needed.

The nectar in the flower attracts the bees. The bees are brushed with pollen when they buzz around the blossom, and they spread it to the next flower that they visit.

That way, the flowers are fertilized, and inside the flower the seeds are produced.

The petals fall off the flower, and what's left, the ovary, then starts to swell—that's the beginning of an apple-to-be. And inside it are tiny seeds. If they were ever planted one day, they would make new trees.

It takes ten to twenty weeks for the apples to reach full size and ripen. By August, the limbs of the tree are chock-full of fruit.

Eventually it's harvest time—time to pick the apples
before they fall to the ground and spoil.

At some orchards you can pick your own.

Some apples will be squeezed in presses for apple juice and apple cider.

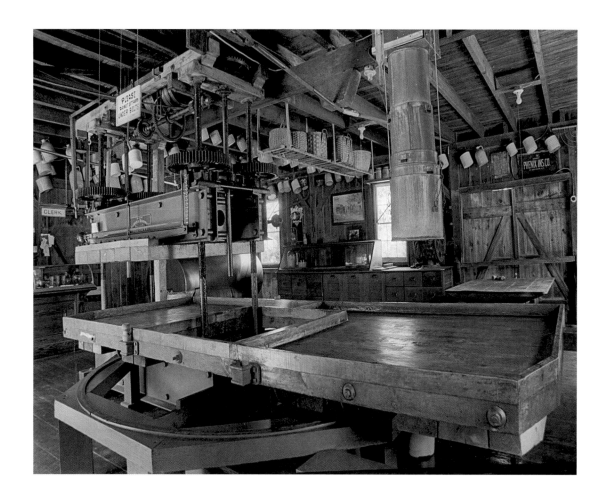

This apple press is nearly one hundred years old.

Some apples will be peeled and sliced and sugared
and spiced . . . and baked into a pie.

Some are fated to be cored and quartered and tossed
into a pot to make applesauce.

And some will just be taken in the hand—perhaps
rubbed on a shirtfront for polish and, with a wonderful
crisp and crunchy sound, munched all around and
swallowed down.

More About Apples

There are other ways that we enjoy apples.

We can eat them in strudel and cobblers, in dumplings and fritters, and baked in cakes. We spread them on bread as apple butter. We have them jellied and fried, sliced and dried. In addition to apple cider, there are apple juice and apple brandy. We cook with vinegar made from apples. Bobbing for apples is messy fun.

And there are still more ways that we use apples—not for eating, but in our speech.

Men, we say, have "Adam's apples"—it's that funny lump in the front of their throats.

Sometimes we say we're "apple-cheeked," when our faces are looking all red from the cold. Today, when we say, "You're the apple of my eye," it means you're something very special to me. And "apple-polishing" is what we call the behavior of people who are always looking for favors.

People say, "An apple a day keeps the doctor away." You know that's not really true, but apples do make healthy food.

And people say, "Apples don't fall too far from the tree." They mean that children are bound to behave more or less as their parents do. What do you think? Could that be true?

And people say, "One bad apples spoils the rest." Just one wormy apple in a whole basketful, and pretty soon they're all no good. Sometimes they call a person "a bad apple" and by that they mean, "He's not only evil, he makes others bad." Do you think one bad person can make others bad?

Apples show up in history, too, and in the stories that people told a long time ago.

The most famous apple of all was the one forbidden to Adam and Eve. The story goes that when they ate the apple from the forbidden tree, they started all of the world's woes.

Then there's the story about a Greek goddess named Eris. She was looking for trouble, so here's what she did: She got a golden apple and wrote on it, "FOR THE MOST BEAUTIFUL," and left it around where three other goddesses were bound to see it. You know how jealous goddesses can be. They found a young prince and demanded that he decide which one of them deserved to have the apple. He gave it to Aphrodite, the goddess of love, but the other two goddesses got really sore, so they went and started the Trojan War.

Another Greek story concerns Atalanta. She promised to take for a mate any man she could not beat in a race. Now, that wasn't exactly fair, because she was the fastest runner anywhere. And Hippomenes loved her, but he didn't stand a chance. So he asked Aphrodite (the same goddess of love) to give him a hand. She gave him three golden apples, and during the race, whenever Atalanta got ahead, he would throw one her way. Atalanta stopped to grab each one. Now you tell me which runner won.

In 1307, in Switzerland, William Tell, as a test of his skill, was forced to shoot, with an arrow, an apple off his own son's head. It was a terrible risk to force him to take; a terrible price if he didn't succeed. He took his crossbow, and you can bet he aimed it carefully. He shot the apple, his son was saved, and he is a Swiss hero to this very day.

In the middle of the nineteenth century there was Johnny Appleseed. That was the name given to John Chapman, who so believed in the goodness of apples that he traveled by foot all over the land, planting the seeds of apple trees that he himself would never see.

Apples come in many different kinds. Here are just a few of people's favorites. See if you can tell which one is mine.

Braeburn

Cameo

Cortland

Fuji

Golden Delicious

Granny Smith

McIntosh

Red Delicious

Gala

DATE DUE

DEMCO